TALES
FROM THE
TOWPATH

For Hannah

TALES FROM THE TOWPATH

STORIES AND HISTORIES OF
THE COTSWOLD CANALS

FIONA EADIE

ILLUSTRATED BY TRACY SPIERS

The
History
Press

Fiona Eadie is a Gloucestershire-based storyteller and deviser of storywalks through the landscape. She is passionate about language, about bringing the spoken word to life and uncovering stories of place.

The original tales in this book are complemented by the evocative illustrations of local artist Tracy Spiers.

First published 2018

The History Press
The Mill, Brimscombe Port
Stroud, Gloucestershire, GL5 2QG
www.thehistorypress.co.uk

British Library Cataloguing in Publication Data.
A catalogue record for this book is available from the British Library.

ISBN 978 0 7509 8767 7

Typesetting and origination by The History Press
Printed and bound in Great Britain by TJ Books Limited, Padstow, Cornwall

CONTENTS

ACKNOWLEDGEMENTS

I am very grateful for all the assistance and encouragement that I have been given in the researching and compiling of this book.

David Marshall and Stroud District Council (SDC) were central in bringing seven of these stories into being and deserve much of the credit. SDC commissioned me to devise a series of towpath story walks when it was the body leading the restoration of the canals, which was largely funded by the Heritage Lottery Fund. I then told the stories to schoolchildren on educational visits organised by the Cotswold Canals Trust (CCT). I am delighted that the tales now have a permanent home in this collection.

Lois Francis, and Clive and Jill Field, have been wonderful sources of information and encouragement, and I am grateful for the time and the material they have given me. I am also extremely grateful to Jill Field for her skilled proofreading and inspired suggestions. I appreciate

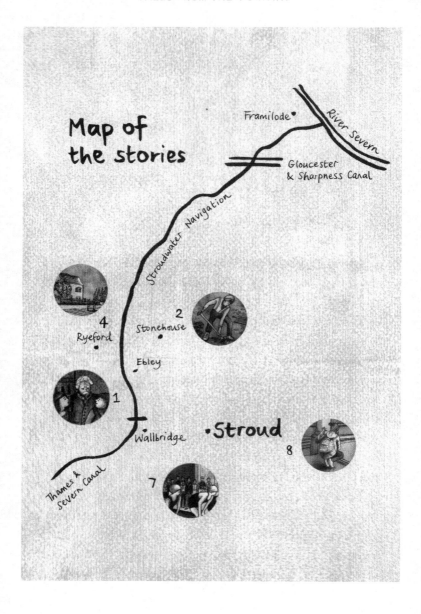

Map of the stories

Framilode

River Severn

Gloucester & Sharpness Canal

Stroudwater Navigation

4
Ryeford

2
Stonehouse

Ebley

1

Wallbridge

•Stroud

8

7

Thames & Severn Canal

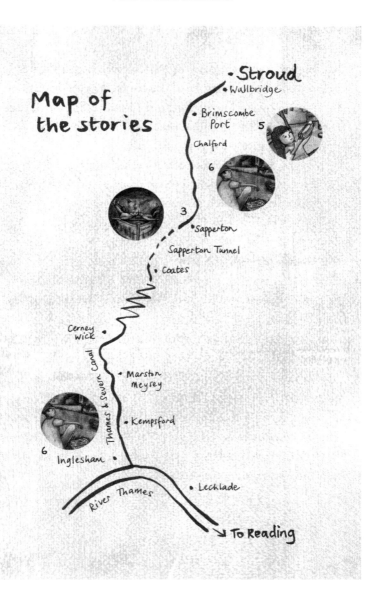

Map of
the stories

• **Stroud**
• Wallbridge
• Brimscombe Port
5
Chalford
6
3
• Sapperton
Sapperton Tunnel
• Coates
Cerney Wick
Thames & Severn Canal
• Marston Meysey
• Kempsford
6
Inglesham
• Lechlade
River Thames
→ **To Reading**

the support of others associated with CCT, including Paul Weller.

Hugh Conway Jones has generously and unfailingly advised me on all manner of canal history queries. I have been awed by his knowledge and I am indebted to Hugh for his detailed reading of each chapter. Any errors that remain are entirely my responsibility.

My good friend Rosie Simpson accompanied me on early expeditions to possible story sites and was helpful and perceptive in talking over ideas.

I am delighted with the evocative illustrations that Tracy Spiers has created, which bring the settings and the characters to life, and I have appreciated Tracy's skill, patience and good humour. My thanks also go to her models – Roger, Megan, Rosie and Kezia Spiers, and Bruce Baker.

I also want to thank Paul and Jo Hofman for their patient and skilled work in making a promotional video of the Samuel the Navvy story (*see* https://www.youtube.com/watch?v=OcmBD5Lqhvc).

I have been helped in many different ways by Kirsty Hartsiotis, Anthony Nanson, Val Kirby, Hugh Barton, Jane Bethell, Mike Rust, Jim Pentney, Paul Pennycook, and the Gloucestershire Archive.

INTRODUCTION

This book was written at a pivotal time in the history of the Cotswold canals. It is the year in which Prince Charles opened Wallbridge Lower Lock to mark the re-joining of the two canals – the Stroudwater and the Thames and Severn – and the completion of an amazing piece of restoration work involving 6 miles of canal, ten locks and eight new bridges.

The long-term plans for further phases of restoration are inspired and ambitious, and will, when completed, once again see canals linking the Severn and the Thames. For all these reasons, this is a great time to honour the canals' past … and their future.

It seems to me that the local history of where we live or of the places we choose to visit is a vital part of what we experience there. It contributes, in ways seen and unseen, to the sense of place.

The eight stories in this book evoke aspects of life on both canals, from their beginnings in the eighteenth century up to today and beyond. I am impressed by the power of story to illuminate history and the power of the imagination to engage with historical details/truths through stories, which then lodge them in the mind and the memory. So, as readers and listeners, we can sit comfortably in our chairs in the twenty-first century while picturing scenes in our imagination that temporarily transport us back or forward to quite another time. In the best instances, when the story is over, a certain understanding and feeling for that era lingers on.

As the two waterways wind their way from Framilode on the Severn through the Cotswolds to Inglesham on the Thames, passing through towns, villages and countryside, they hold the stories of all who lived and worked on them. A vast and numberless company of navvies, lock-keepers, lengthsmen, leggers, boatmen and women, boat-builders, proprietors, merchants, swimmers and many others have their tales to tell and it is some of these that I have tried to capture in the stories. In doing so, I have interwoven fact with fiction – daily life as it would have been, interrupted by, say, a dream or a fish with fins of gold!

So, each of the characters and their adventures are fictional* – for example, neither Amos the lock-keeper

---

* With the exception of Benjamin Grazebrook, a very real man, who played an important role in the creating of the Stroudwater Navigation.

nor Jim the bargeman ever existed – but the details of their daily lives are rooted in truth and fact. A lock-keeper might well have worried about his parents going into the workhouse, and there was a period when a young man with ambition could have taken a cargo by barge from Chalford all the way to Inglesham.

Some of the tales are set on the Stroudwater Navigation: Amos the lock-keeper at Ryeford Double Lock, Samuel the navvy in his hovel near Stonehouse, Benjamin Grazebrook at Far Hill overlooking Wallbridge, Elizabeth practising her swimming near Cainscross and Anna growing up in Stroud; while others take place along the Thames and Severn: Jack legging barges through the Sapperton Tunnel, Jim transporting timber from Chalford to Inglesham and Kate celebrating life around the Bourne near Brimscombe Port.

The stories stand alone – each one an episode drawing on real life with a folk tale at its heart – and, at the end of each, I have included notes that may help to set the story in its historical context. Seven of them were originally commissioned by Stroud District Council and written as a series of story walks for educational visits to the Cotswold Canals Trust – a way to engage both young people and adults with local history. Each relates to a specific time and place (see maps on pp. 8 & 9). Now they can be read at home or out and about in the places mentioned. You can, for example, still drink in a pub at the end of the Sapperton Tunnel just as Jack did in 1802, then walk to one of the grand entrances and imagine him in there legging a barge through the pitch darkness.

For 150 years the Cotswold canals played an important part in the history of Stroud and also that of Stonehouse, Chalford, Coates and all the other places on the 36-mile route from the Severn to the Thames. The building of the canals contributed to the landscape and connected the settlements along their banks with the wider world. They were then abandoned, faded from sight and are now returning to centre stage.

Who are these stories for? They are for all who know and love the Cotswold canals – for those who live nearby, those who make frequent visits to the waterways and those who are discovering them for the first time. They are also for those who know Stroud and other canalside towns of old, who may even remember the canals before they were abandoned, as well as those who have watched or are involved in their skilled and impressive restoration. It is for the children of the Stroud valleys and further afield who are studying local history, who might like a glimpse of what life was like on the canals in earlier times and who may, with luck, become champions of the canals in the future.

These stories are also for all the walkers, canoeists, cyclists, runners and fishermen who presently enjoy the canal and its towpaths, as well as the many boaters who will do so in the future. My hope is that these stories will inspire readers to seek out the places in which they are set.

The tales are here to entertain, to give glimpses into the past and the future and to honour those who went before.

I enjoyed walking the towpaths as I planned this book, following the Stroudwater Navigation and the beginning of the Thames and Severn canal past modern houses and old mills, green fields and wooded hillsides. Accompanied at times by the river, the railway and all manner of roads, lanes and byways, I travelled a looping route through the landscape, stitched in place by locks and bridges and home to a wealth of wildlife including ducks and swans, otters, kingfishers, herons and dragonflies.

There are, undoubtedly, many other tales from the towpath yet to be told – other stories for another time – but if Samuel digging out the Stroudwater Navigation in the 1770s, or Elizabeth swimming for all she is worth in the Thames and Severn more than a century and a half later, can help to bring the history of these wonderful canals to life, I will be more than pleased.

Fiona Eadie, 2018

1

Benjamin Grazebrook, Canal Pioneer, 1700s

A GRANDFATHER TELLS HOW THE STROUDWATER
NAVIGATION CAME ABOUT

The children – Henry who was 8 years old and Emma, 6 – looked out of the window of the carriage and counted the mills along the road to Stroud – tight with excitement as they got nearer and nearer to seeing their grandfather. It was summer and they were on their way from Minchinhampton to spend a few days with their grandparents – a treat they looked forward to every year. This time they were all meeting up at the big house where their uncle Joseph lived and then, they hoped, there would be a visit to the canal.

At length their coachman turned the horses into the driveway of Far Hill and there was grandfather, Benjamin Grazebrook, standing in the doorway of the large, elegant home waiting to welcome them.

They loved this tall, gruff man with his white hair, fine moustache and always – winter or summer – his faded red woollen waistcoat.

Henry and Emma tumbled out of the carriage into his arms.

'Well my lovely ones, how good it is to see you – I think you are as glad to visit your grandfather as I am to have you here. What walks we'll have, what stories I have to tell you.'

'Tell us one now, a true one,' said Emma. 'The one about the old woman and the red cloth.'

'In a bit, there's no hurry. Come along in now, say hello to your grandmother and your uncle Joseph and have some luncheon.'

After lunch, Benjamin proposed a walk down to the canal but their grandmother protested. 'Don't take the children down to the canal Benjamin. It's not fitting, very rough and dangerous and they'll get all dusty.'

'Anne,' said grandfather. 'It's an important part of their heritage. If I don't show them and tell them about it, who will? Nothing you can say – dust or no dust – will stop me.'

'You're a stubborn man, Benjamin Grazebrook – always have been and always will be.'

So, just as Henry and Emma had hoped, the three of them set out on a walk, and as always they went down to the canal – the Stroudwater Navigation – which, to them, was the best thing about every visit to their beloved grandfather.

They knew that he – Benjamin Grazebrook – had been a very important person in making it all happen. He had been a proprietor – one of the Company of Proprietors of the Stroudwater Navigation – and it was because of all his hard work that Stroud had its canal.

What grandfather loved best was to walk from Wallbridge out towards Stonehouse, asking the children questions all the way and giving them brass coins if they got the answers right. Once he had even given Henry a silver shilling.

They stopped by the lock at Wallbridge.

'What was here when I first came to Stroud, Henry?'

'Nothing sir, no canal at all, just the River Frome winding along, too shallow for cargo boats.'

'Good lad, and now, Emma, why do we need a canal?'

'For us and the mills,' said the little girl. 'The barges bring coal for our fires and corn for us to eat, and they take away ... umm ... well, lots of other things. They bring money to Stroud and make it an important place.'

'That's it, well done.'

'Have you got lots of money grandfather?'

Benjamin laughed. 'Well I have now but I didn't always have. When I was a young man, I started out as a plumber and that didn't make me rich but it did mean I knew about water and I saw how important water transport was – it was the future and I worked hard for years and years persuading everyone that we needed this canal. It wasn't easy.'

Just then, amid all the busy traffic on the canal they spotted a trow, the *Endeavour*, approaching the lock – on its way to Brimscombe Port with a cargo of salt. The skipper recognised the older man and doffed his cap.

'Morning Mr Grazebrook sir.'

'Good morning Peter – good to see you and your fine boat still working. I remember when the Company hired the *Endeavour* and you sailed her across the Severn to the Forest of Dean to get the hard stone we needed to make the coping stones for the locks. It was a rough crossing wasn't it Peter – we nearly lost you and the cargo.'

'That it was sir, very rough, I remember it well.'

From Wallbridge they turned and walked west towards a most impressive stone building.

'What's this Emma?'

'Lodgemore Mill.'

'And what do they make here?'

Henry jumped in. 'The red cloth grandfather, the Stroud Scarlet cloth for the soldiers and ... your coat. Will you tell us the story now?'

'Oh very well, let's go and sit down.'

The three of them sat down on a bench beside the mill in the afternoon sunshine.

'Are you sure you want the same old story again?'

'Yes, yes grandfather.'

'Well this is how it happened – a long time ago now. When I was first clerk to the Company of Proprietors, I went to see the mill owners at Lodgemore Mill to tell them how much better their business would do once we had a canal from the Severn to Stroud. They were worried it would take the water they needed to turn the mill wheels. I knew this wasn't the case and I did my best to reassure them. As a gesture of goodwill I bought a length of their special cloth – Stroud Scarlet – after the meeting thinking that I would have a fine coat made from it.

'On the way home that evening, my mind was full of the meeting and I was wondering how and if this canal was ever going to get built … then the strangest thing happened. An old woman came out of the shadows and touched my arm. She seemed very, very old, her face lined and creased like an ancient map but her voice was clear and her eyes were bright as they looked into mine: "You will get your canal Benjamin, never fear, but not before that cloth you carry is almost worn out." I went to reply but just as suddenly as she had appeared she disappeared and there was no one there.

'Well I took the cloth home and your grandmother had it made up into the finest coat. How proud I felt when I put it on – quite the gentleman I looked – and somehow it gave me the confidence to keep pushing for a canal for Stroud.

'I wore it to all the Company of Proprietors' meetings, I wore it to the meeting where we set up Stroud's own bank. I wore it here, I wore it there, I even wore it, well some of it, to the Battle of Carter's Close.'

'Tell us about that,' said Henry.

'In a bit, I will, let's walk a little more now.'

Henry helped pull grandfather to his feet and they continued on their way. There was no towpath beside the canal in those days – just fields with deep ruts etched by the men, the horses and the donkeys that trudged along them with long ropes attached to the boats they were hauling. The trows had sails but they couldn't use these on the busy canal with all its locks. The children watched the trows and the canal barges pass with their cargoes of coal, wood, iron and salt. They stared as the sweaty bowhaulers struggled passed them grunting, pulling their heavy loads. The canal and its banks were a busy place and Henry and Emma found it hard to imagine there had been a time when it wasn't here.

When, dusty and thirsty, they reached the locks at Dudbridge, the lock-keeper greeted grandfather warmly. 'You and the young ones could do with a drink I dare say?' and they all nodded.

He invited them into his little vegetable garden, sat them down on a bench under the pear tree and presently his wife appeared with a jug of elderflower drink and three glasses. She smiled at them shyly and went back inside.

'The Battle of Carter's Close, tell us about it grandfather.'

Benjamin took a swig of the elderflower and began.

'Well by the time I was in my 40s there had been several plans for the canal – none of which had really worked. Then, in 1775, things definitely got going. The company began cutting out the canal at Framilode – at a place called Carter's Close – where it would join the Severn. We employed twenty-seven men as cutters – navvies they were called later because they worked on the navigation – and with their pickaxes and their shovels they dug and cut and wheeled the earth away. They were so strong these men and the work was hard and dangerous.'

The children knew what happened next. Some people were excited and pleased about the canal work but others were not. Some of the landowners and some of the mill owners didn't want the canal to go through their land. They thought, they worried, that their fields would be damaged by water oozing through the canal banks. They said they weren't being paid enough for the land and they thought that, when the canal was filled, it would leave their mills short of water.

'Now,' said grandfather. 'There was a Mr John Purnell and he wasn't at all happy, he was angry. He had a mill making tin plate at Framilode and he said that Carter's Close belonged to him. One day he just sent his man with a message to the cutters saying they should stop work immediately. But the cutters carried on and they started digging out Framilode Lock. Two days later he came back and said, "Stop this work at once", and he put up two notices forbidding them to continue.'

'What did you do grandfather?' asked Emma

'I travelled out to see what all the fuss was about and I told the men to get back to work. Not long after that we had a celebration to mark the laying of the first stone of Framilode Lock – a big party; we even buried some coins under the stone and we thought all was well.'

'Did you wear your red coat grandfather?'

'Well I did, part of it at least. You see by now I'd had that red coat for more than twenty years and it had got a bit worn so your grandmother had it cut down and altered to make a fine jacket. I still wore it here and there with great pride.

'Not long after the party the real trouble began. Purnell and others said we had no right in law to build a canal; we were only allowed to make the river navigable. Every day the cutters would dig out the canal and every night, under cover of darkness, Purnell's men would fill it in again. There were lots of fights I can tell you between the cutters and the fillers and it got pretty violent.

'In the end we went to the court of law in London and they said Purnell was right and we had to stop the canal building altogether. Oh I was annoyed and tired of the whole business. When I got back from London it was evening and, as I walked home – in my red jacket – it was getting dark. Suddenly there was a tug on my arm and there again was the old woman I'd seen years before. Her face was lined, her voice was strong and her eyes were bright. She told me, "You will get your canal Benjamin, never fear, but not before the red cloth you wear is almost worn out."

'And then she vanished.'

Benjamin told the children how this second visit from the old woman gave him the determination to carry on and to see the whole canal plan through.

'After that,' he said, 'we worked and worked until we got a whole new Act of Parliament saying we could build a canal and the cutting work began again. It took three years to dig out the whole 8 miles of the canal and all twelve locks but we got there in the end.'

'And did you ever see the old woman again?' asked Henry.

'Just once …'

Benjamin got to his feet, it was late in the afternoon now and they started the walk back to Far Hill. And as they walked he told them about the wonderful day – more than ten years ago but as fresh in his mind as if it had been yesterday – that had marked the grand opening of the canal.

'I wanted to look very smart for that wonderful occasion,' he told them, 'but by that time, my red jacket was beginning to look shabby and worn. Your grandmother said, "Never mind, we can use the best of the cloth and make you a fine waistcoat."'

Benjamin's eyes sparkled as he told Henry and Emma about how the day had started with a great public breakfast for the people of Stroud held on the bowling green at Cainscross.

'Then guns were fired to mark the start of a procession led by your uncle Joseph ... and there were workmen with their tools and flags and banners and music. They walked all through the town under decorated arches and past buildings hung with brightly coloured cloths. It was spectacular. I wish you could have seen it.'

The children listened happily as their grandfather described the magnificent horse-drawn Venetian pleasure barge that had carried him and other important people down the new navigation from Wallbridge to Ebley Mill and back, followed by a host of other decorated boats.

'Thousands of people lined the banks and, when we got back to Wallbridge, a whole ox had been roasted specially and it was cut up and shared out among the crowd.'

'What happened then grandfather? What happened next?' whispered Emma.

'Well, when it was finally time to leave the celebrations, I set off through noisy, laughing groups of people towards home. I hadn't gone very far when suddenly there was a tug on my arm and there again was the old woman. Her face was lined, her voice was strong and her eyes were bright.

'"You got your canal Benjamin and now the red cloth you wear is almost worn out."

'So,' said the old man beaming at his grandchildren, 'in the end the old woman was right.'

Emma smiled up at him. She loved that story, she loved listening to her grandfather telling it but now, looking at him standing there with his thumbs tucked into the pockets of his waistcoat, she suddenly realised something for the first time.

'Oh grandfather you still wear it don't you? You always wear that old red waistcoat and now I know why,' said Emma.

NOTES

In the eighteenth century Stroud was renowned for its fine woollen cloth, especially the celebrated Stroud Scarlet from which Benjamin has his coat made in this story.

As the demand for Stroud cloth grew, the powerful and influential local clothiers needed better transport to and from the mills because the roads were poor even in good weather and almost impassable in the depths of winter. Coal was also needed in large quantities for the town's rapidly growing population. Many believed that a canal linking Stroud and the Severn would solve these problems, while others were bitterly opposed to the idea.

The story is set in 1798, when Benjamin Grazebrook was 67 years old, although it describes the period from the 1750s onwards.

Benjamin (1731–1810) played a very important role in the building of the Stroudwater Navigation. He began his working life as a plumber, became a clerk to the canal's Company of Proprietors and ended up as their main surveyor.

His entrepreneurial skills were many and Benjamin was shrewd, successful and a good negotiator. In addition to becoming a partner in Stroud's first bank – which became Grazebrook and Company – and the Stroud Brewery, he also ran a canal carrying company with his own small fleet of boats trading between Stroud, Gloucester and Bristol.

As Benjamin's success grew, he became a very wealthy man, invested a great deal of money in the canal and had a grand house – Far Hill – built for him. It stood on the site now occupied by Homebase on the Cainscross Road until it was demolished in the 1980s. This elegant Stroud home overlooked the canal with gardens running down to the water. By the time of this story, it had become the home of one of his sons, Joseph Grazebrook.

Benjamin and his wife Anne had three other children who survived to adulthood and one of these, their daughter Mary, was the mother of Henry and Emma.

Lodgemore Mill, where Benjamin stops to tell the children the first instalment of his story, has been making cloth since the fifteenth century. Today, its products include tennis ball covers as seen at Wimbledon and cloth used on the tables of the World Snooker tournaments.

Bowhaulers were men who pulled the vessels along the canal in the days before the canal had a proper towpath.

The Battle of Carter's Close really did take place and was part of what was later referred to as a 'malignant spirit of opposition' to the canal. Several months before the 'battle', when it became apparent that the canal proprietors intended to proceed, certain landowners and mill owners established a subscription fund to oppose the navigation and met to discuss their plans in the George Inn at Frocester.

2

SAMUEL THE NAVVY, 1777

THE LIFE OF A LABOURER DIGGING THE CANAL INTO BEING

In the year 1777 the hard labour of digging out the Stroudwater Navigation from Framilode to Stroud was under way.

Samuel's life was not an easy one – in fact it was harder than you or I can possibly imagine. He rose at first light from the pile of blankets in his hovel beside the river Frome near Stonehouse, where he was living with his wife Ellen and the children. He staggered outside, seized his pick and shovel and joined the other men making their way to the deep, muddy trench that would one day be a canal.

'A navvy, that's what they call me,' he'd explained to his young daughter, Beth, when they first arrived there. 'Navvy from navigator see because when I'm out all day working my darling, I'm digging, digging, digging – digging out a navigation, this one right here which will, when it's done, stretch all the way from the River Severn to Stroud town.'

Right now, his back, his arms and his legs still ached from the day before, he was hungry and his clothes were crumpled and dirty – he slept in them because he didn't have any others. But he was a strong man was Samuel – stronger probably than anyone you might come across today – and he'd been working his way from one canal to another for many years now.

When he wasn't digging he was puddling – cold work that made his feet turn blue and ache. The canal was lined with puddle to make it watertight. Puddle is wet clay squashed down to force all the air bubbles out and make it waterproof. First the trench or cut would be lined with clay brought on carts and shovelled into place. Then the wet clay would be trampled and packed down hard by the feet of the navvies or by driving sheep and cattle up and down the canal. As long as the clay stayed wet, the puddle lining sealed the canal bed and stopped the water from leaking away.

When he got there, some of the other navvies were already hard at work. He could smell mud and clay and sweat and he could hear the shouts as the men in the trench – who had filled wooden barrows with soil – shouted to the others up above to start moving the horses that would drag the barrows to the surface.

Samuel was one of the best navvies, one of the most experienced and one of the hardest working. When he got down to work he could dig out a trench 9 metres long, 1 metre wide and 1 metre deep in a day – shifting 9 cubic metres of earth using just his strength and a shovel and pickaxe. His hands were as tough as old leather and calloused all across the palms from using the shovel day in and day out.

'All right Bill,' he said to one of the others when he got down into the trench.

'Right Sam, glad it's dry in here and there's no sign of rain. Sunday tomorrow.'

And they both grinned. Sunday was the only day they had off and Samuel had plans to go fishing. Little did he know what his fishing trip would bring.

All that day long, the gang of navvies dug in their trench. When a barrow was filled, Samuel would struggle onto the wooden planks that led up to the surface and he'd hold the barrow handles firmly while the horse at the top pulled it slowly up. The work was dangerous – it was all too easy to slip and lose your footing on the greasy, muddy planks. Then man and barrow full of earth and rocks would career over into the trench, hurting themselves and those working below.

When it finally got to the end of the day and the men were paid, Samuel, unlike most of the others, didn't go straight to the inn and spend his wages on beer. Instead he went home, handed over the money to his wife Ellen, who bought the family's food, and then, after a good wash in the cold river water and a plate of stew, he fell into an exhausted sleep.

What did they eat, this poor family? Well a rough sort of bread, eels, ducks' eggs, even moorhen eggs when they could get them, the young shoots of hops from the hedgerows and vegetables begged from kitchen gardens. Any fish that Samuel caught made a welcome change to his family's diet and he had his eye on a place further up river where the water pooled deeply and he fancied there might be a perch or two lurking.

It was a bright, summer's morning when he awoke. The sun had risen and he could hear a lark singing high up in the blue. Ellen was already up and preparing a coarse porridge of oats and water. 'Here Samuel – have a fill of this before you set off and mind you catch us some good 'uns – a salmon or a trout would do just fine.'

Samuel laughed, gave her a hug and set off with his wooden rod, string and a jar of maggots as bait. When he reached the pool, which was deep with steep, slippery banks, he carefully found a secure place to sit – like many navvies he couldn't swim and he didn't fancy trying to scramble up the muddy sides if he fell in. During the long, peaceful morning he caught two trout – enough to give his family a treat but there was no sign of any perch.

He was just about to give up and make his way back home when there was a tug on the line and, jerking it up, he saw a fine young perch struggling to get free.

He was amazed – this was no ordinary fish. Its scales were silver and shimmered and shone, while along its back the fins were as golden as the sunlight. Samuel stared and then took hold of it and freed it from the line while it writhed and twisted in his hands, its mouth opening and shutting – desperate to be back in the water.

You are something special – quite a beauty indeed. I'd like to show you to my family but I don't want one as fine as you to die. And with that thought, Samuel threw the fish back into the water and watched as it plunged down out of sight.

'Yes father, a large perch with silver scales and golden fins … of course we believe you!' laughed the children later when he told them what he'd seen. All fishermen talk about the one that got away and they were not at all sure about this yarn their father was spinning, but they tucked into the fish pie Ellen had cooked with delight.

The next few weeks and months continued much as before. The weather turned wet and cold as autumn set in and the digging was harder than ever. Often Samuel's hands, ears and nose were blue with cold and the thin, poor clothes he wore did little to help. He had old work trousers made of corduroy, an ancient frayed shirt, a bright neckerchief that had seen better days and a cloth cap worn sideways on.

But it wasn't just the cold and the work that made life difficult. The longer the navvies were in the area, the more the local people disliked them. Some of the navvies were rough, many drank too much and a few stole things, but others, like Samuel, were honest, hard-working men. The locals said they were all a bad lot, good for nothing except fighting and drinking. Anything that went missing was blamed on the navvies and they were often met with insults and curses.

Late one grey November afternoon, Samuel was on his way home along the path beside the river – just near the pool where he had caught the perch – when he saw a group of drunken young men coming towards him. They were clearly angry and looking for trouble.

'Evening,' he said as they approached.

'Dirty navvy,' said one of them spitting at him, 'Dirty, thieving navvy – what you doing out alone? Poaching I bet, stealing from honest folk,' and he poked Samuel in the chest. 'Your sort should go back where you came from, we don't want you here.'

The others jostled round and Samuel, angry, was just about to lash out when one of them shoved him hard from behind and he lost his footing and fell down the slippery bank into the deep river pool. He shouted, yelled to them that he couldn't swim, but they just ran off laughing. He struggled and splashed trying to keep his head above the surface but swallowing great mouthfuls of cold, muddy water as he panicked. Samuel was about to sink under for the second time when he felt something solid and strong swim alongside him. Even in the gloom he could see exactly what it was – a large perch, no ordinary fish. Its scales were silver and shimmered and shone while along its back the fins were as golden as sunlight.

Hardly aware of what he was doing, Samuel held on to the perch's fins and it guided him to a place on the bank where there were footholds that he could use to scramble up to safety. As he stood shivering on the bank, spluttering water from his lungs, he looked down and saw the large fish plunge back into the depths and disappear.

This time, when he told his astonished family what had happened they believed him because, stuck to his dripping shirt, was a small patch of shimmering silver scales.

NOTES

Navvies like Samuel were probably not recruited locally but hired when they finished work on other navigations such as the Midland canals. They worked in teams or gangs.

Samuel would have worked a six-day week for a wage of around 10*s* (50 pence in today's money). However, many contractors also hired unskilled farm workers because, initially at least, they could be paid less than the professional navvies and were keen for work that was regular and better paid than that on the land. The farm workers had to learn excavation skills on the job and it took several months to achieve the speed and skill of experienced navvies. Many who began as labourers on one canal might then move to another and spend most of their lives, like Samuel did, digging waterways.

Navvies were a migrant workforce and, at the time of this story when canal building was gaining in pace, their numbers were growing fast. By the end of the eighteenth century, it is estimated that the workforce numbered some 50,000 men.

The navvies achieved incredible feats of engineering using only shovels, picks and barrows, the odd bit of dynamite and a great deal of strength and muscle power. All in all they built more than 2,000 miles of canals in Britain.

In this story, Samuel is working on the Stroudwater Navigation, which opened in 1779 and continued in operation until the Act for Abandonment of Navigation in 1954. He and the other navvies created an 8-mile long canal with twelve locks. At first the main trade was largely in coal, which was needed for the prosperous Stroud woollen trade. Transporting coal by water was much cheaper, more reliable and more efficient than carrying such bulky loads by road. A single horse could haul about 1 ton a day on land but it could haul up to 60 tons if harnessed to a barge on water.

The digging out of the last canals and the creating of the earliest railways overlapped in time and so, from the end of the 1820s onwards, many men would have moved from one to the other and continued their itinerant life as railway navvies.

3

JACK THE LEGGER, 1802

MOVING BARGES THROUGH THE SAPPERTON TUNNEL

'Oh my back aches, oh my backside aches!' moaned Jack as he stumbled off the barge and into the New Inn at Coates.

For the last three hours Jack had been lying on his back, on a narrow, hard piece of wood, moving a barge full of timber through an inky black tunnel by walking his legs along the side walls.

A 'legger', that was what Jack was and that described his work. He was 37 years old and unmarried. His face was broad and weather-beaten under his battered black felt hat, he wasn't particularly tall and his back was slightly bent from the hours he spent 'legging'. He wore the usual clothes of his kind – a tattered shirt and old jacket, corduroy trousers tied with string under the knee and heavy worn leather boots.

Jack and his mate Lucky worked together – one on each side of the barge – and it was exhausting, tedious work. Dangerous as well – many a legger had tumbled into the black waters of the tunnel and many had drowned.

Jack had lived near Sapperton all his life – in fact, his grandfather Thomas had been one of the men who built the Sapperton Tunnel – and, when he wasn't legging, Jack made his living doing odds and ends. Sometimes he did a bit of farm work, sometimes he helped haul the canal barges along but a lot of the time he sat in the inn – either the New Inn at Coates or the Bricklayers Arms at the Sapperton end – smoking his clay pipe, drinking ale and waiting for the next boat that needed leggers. It was dark in the inn, dark and comfortable, and it smelt of tobacco, ale and onions.

That morning, a sturdy barge, *Fortune*, had moored up at the Bricklayers Arms; she was a strong boat made of oak with an open hold full of timber. The cabin was brightly painted with roses and castles and she was pulled along by two grey donkeys attached to her by long ropes and harnesses. The skipper came in, ordered an ale and looked around the smoky inn.

'Where you headin' fur?' asked Jack.

'Cirencester with a load of timber. I need leggers.'

'Well me and Lucky, we're available,' said Jack – his mate Lucky stopped chewing his lump of baccy and nodded.

'Good,' said the skipper. 'We'll see you at the tunnel entrance shortly.'

After the skipper had drunk down his ale, he went back to the *Fortune,* untied the ropes and his boy urged their two donkeys – Stubborn and Patience – to start pulling the barge on down the canal. It wasn't far to the start of the tunnel and, just as they reached it, Jack and Lucky came hurrying along the towpath behind them. Ahead was the dark, damp, dripping tunnel.

'Well,' said the boy. 'I'll take Stubborn and Patience on over the top now and I'll see you at the other end.'

'Yes,' said the skipper. 'Make sure they graze a bit and rest a bit ready for the long haul to Cirencester.'

Jack was carrying a flat piece of wood nearly as wide as the tunnel itself, which he placed across the front of the barge so that it stuck out on either side. Then he and Lucky huffed and puffed their way into position until they lay with their heads nearly touching, their hands clutching the sides of the board and their feet on the walls of the tunnel.

By working together and in time, they could keep the barge moving through the dark tunnel. The only noise was the drip, drip, drip of water from the roof, the tramp of hard, nailed boots on the walls and the heavy, laboured breathing of the two men. A candle gave a little light and cast eerie shadows all around but beyond its glow all was pitch black as they slowly made their way through the centre of Sapperton Hill. The journey took three hours. It was very hard work.

'Tell us about your grandfather,' said Lucky. 'You know, the "dommed if it worn't story" … I like that one.'

'Alright,' huffed Jack, glad to have something to take his mind off his aching legs.

'Well, my grandfather Thomas worked on making this tunnel when he was about my age – if you think this is dangerous work, Lucky, you should hear what he did. Lowered every morning, down by basket, into a great shaft, a great hole in the ground, working all day digging out the tunnel, blasting the rock with black powder and then clearing away the rubble. Day after day, deep underground for very little pay, living in a tent, sweating and dirty and tired.'

'Hmm, I'm sweating and dirty,' said Lucky. 'S'pose at least we get to lie down,' he cackled.

'Yes well,' Jack carried on, 'when this tunnel was built it was the longest in the world and grandfather was really proud of what he and the other navvies had made. When it were nearly finished – 1788 – when the whole length of it were nearly done, the King himself, His Majesty George III, came to see it. Grandfather was determined to be there for the occasion, so he washed himself in the canal, put on a clean neckerchief and was hurrying along the path towards Coates when he met a very smartly dressed gentleman coming the other way.

"Where are you going my man?" he says to grandfather.

"To see the King, sir, aren't you going that way yourself?" says grandfather.

"The King," said the smart gentleman, ignoring grandfather's question, "I know him well."

"You know him sir! I could tell you weren't from round here but, well I never. Are you a gentleman of the court sir?"

"You could say that," said the smart gentleman smiling and, when grandfather looked at him in awe, like, he continued in a matter of fact sort of way. "It just so happens that I am the King."

'And he took a shining guinea from his waistcoat pocket and gave it to grandfather who, a bit bewildered, took it and walked on. After a few yards he stopped and looked at the head on the coin ...

"Well," he says to himself. "I'm dommed if it worn't!"

Lucky chortled. 'It's all true, isn't it Jack?'

'True as I'm lying here Lucky. It's a great story in our family is that one, I even remember seeing the shining guinea when I was a boy. Now it's your turn ... tell me the story about Fred ... the one about the hare.'

They had reached the middle of the tunnel and both men were beginning to flag. To take their minds off the mile and a half they still had to travel, Lucky began his story.

'Well, I've been told that there was once, over Siddington way, a young man called Fred who spent all his days dreaming and dozing and not doing much. His father were exasperated and, before he set off for work in the morning, he would stomp up the stairs and shout at Fred, "Oy! Get out of bed!."'

'Quite right,' said Jack. 'Wake him up.'

'Fred wasn't really lazy,' continued Lucky. 'He just didn't know what he was going to do for work and all that. And he was in love … he loved Molly, Farmer Smith's daughter, with all his heart even though he had never said a word to her in his whole life.'

'Foolish numbskull,' said Jack.

'One day, Fred was walking through the fields, swishing his stick and daydreaming when, suddenly, a large hare crossed his path and stopped and looked at him. That got Fred thinking and he started mumbling out loud, "If I could catch this hare and take it to market, I could sell it and, with the money, I could buy a few piglets. Oh yes … and I would feed them up and sell them and, with the money, I would buy a cow. Then I would sell the milk from the cow and buy a bull so as I could build up a herd."'

'Hmm,' said Jack. 'Don't know as that would happen.'

'Sshh,' said Lucky, 'or I won't finish the story before we get to Coates.

'"Now," Fred went on, "when I'd built up a good herd I would go to see Farmer Smith and Molly would be there smiling and I would ask for Molly's hand. Molly would be very pleased to have a handsome, rich husband and Farmer Smith would agree to such a fine son-in-law. So we would be married and move into the big, old farmhouse with all the family.'"

'What about Molly's brothers?' asked Jack.

'I was coming to that,' Lucky replied.

'"All Molly's brothers would go off to war and never return."'

'Well that would be sad,' said Jack.

'Sshh,' said Lucky. 'Listen to the story.'

'"All Molly's brothers would go off to war and never return and, in time, me and Molly would inherit the farmhouse and all the farm. We would be very happy and have five strong, healthy children. But one of them would be a dreamer and, every morning, I would have to stomp up the stairs and shout '**Oy! Get out of bed**!'"'

'Fred was daydreaming so strong that he shouted that out real loud, didn't he?' said Jack.

'Yes,' said Lucky. 'He shouted out, "**Oy! Get out of bed**!" Right there in the middle of the meadow and, of course, when he did that, the hare twitched its ears and bounded off into the long grass. And, as for Fred, well he never saw it again.'

'That was the end of his dreams, foolish numbskull,' said Jack.

'Yes indeed,' replied Lucky, 'and look we are nearly there.'

Now a pinprick of light could be seen way ahead of them and both men sighed with relief. The skipper left off steering for a moment and came and replaced the guttering candle. What with that, the story and the end of the tunnel in sight, both men walked the walls with a final burst of energy and the barge emerged into the sunshine.

Jack and Lucky blinked and scowled in the bright light. The boy was there waiting with the donkeys and he helped moor up. Then the skipper came down the barge with their pay and they staggered to their feet, took the money and – complaining loudly about their backs and their backsides – they staggered off with their board to the warmth of the New Inn.

NOTES

As early canal tunnels did not have towpaths, legging was the only way to get the boats, normally drawn by horses or donkeys, from one end to the other. Although it might have been possible to use a pole to push the boat through, this was forbidden by the canal company, which was concerned about possible damage to the masonry.

Legging was damp, dark, claustrophobic and dangerous work, and it was not unusual for leggers to suffer dizziness, fall into the canal and drown. The skill of the leggers came in getting a rhythm going and keeping the vessel in the centre of the tunnel. In this way they avoided bumping into the sides and maintained an average speed of 1 mile an hour.

The Sapperton Tunnel was one of the civil engineering wonders of the age and took five years to build, from

1784–89. In 1788 when the tunnel was almost complete, George III, who was convalescing at Cheltenham, went with members of the Royal Family to visit the Earl of Bathurst near Cirencester. During this visit he was taken to see the portals at either end of the tunnel. These impressive structures – the neo-classical western portal at Coates and the Gothic eastern portal near the Daneway – can still be seen today, having been faithfully restored by the Cotswold Canals Trust.

The tunnel itself is now impassable due to a number of major roof-falls and blockages but there are still pubs at either end – the Tunnel House Inn at Coates and the Daneway Inn at Sapperton.

4

AMOS THE LOCK-KEEPER, 1836

WORK, WORRIES AND DREAMS OF A NINETEENTH-CENTURY CANAL FAMILY

Amos Herbert knew every lock from Ryeford on the Stroudwater Navigation, where he lived and worked, all the way to Brimscombe Port on the Thames and Severn canal. He could recite them like a chant. He had only been beyond Brimscombe Port once in his life – out to where the canal narrowed – and that was with his father when he was a boy.

Amos was the lock-keeper at Ryeford Double Lock and proud to have such a fine job. He was a lock-keeper, his father had been a lock-keeper before him and his grandfather before that. Now he was training up his boy, John, a fine strong lad who was 14 years old and shared his father's pride in the work.

Lock-keeping was full of responsibilities. Amos had to check the water levels and regulating the flow of water between canal and river was a difficult task – he needed to be patient, vigilant, to know what might go wrong and have the skills to sort things out. Amos kept the canal and towpath clear, greased the paddle gear on the lock gates and also made sure that all the boats coming through – the sturdy sailing trows and the narrowboats – didn't damage the locks or leave the sluices running. He saw to it that they glided in nice and graceful without bashing the walls of the lock or the gates. Sometimes he helped to operate the locks but often the crews on the boats did that themselves. Amos was a strong, wiry man with curly, jet-black hair and a weather-beaten face. He could be very stern when needed but mostly he got on well with all the boat crews that came through his lock.

His house, right beside the lock, was made of brick – weatherproof but cold and somewhat dark inside. Downstairs there was a fire for cooking on and a stone-flagged floor and there were three bedrooms upstairs. Amos lived there with his wife Mary, John their son and their two daughters Charlotte, who was 10 years old, and Martha, who was 8. They also had a dog, Tan.

Amos made a reasonable living. The Company of Proprietors provided him with the lock-keeper's house rent-free and, with help from his wife and children, he kept a good vegetable garden. They also had the best apple tree in those parts. It was an Ashmead's Kernel – full of beautiful blossom in the spring and laden with green-gold fruit in the autumn. So they got by. But Amos was worried about money, nonetheless, on account of his poor old parents who lived nearby. His dad could no longer work and they were struggling to pay the rent on their cottage. If they couldn't pay they might be evicted and have to go and live in the workhouse.

Well our story begins one night when Amos was fast asleep in bed. As he slept a voice spoke to him, saying, 'Go to Brimscombe Port Amos, go to Brimscombe Port.' He awoke with a start and wondered if his wife was trying to tell him something urgent. But Mary was sound asleep beside him, snoring gently. Tan was whimpering softly in his dreams but otherwise there was silence. He looked around the room. It was full of shadows but there was no one else there. *How strange*, he thought, *it must have been a dream*. And he went back to sleep.

The next night the voice spoke to him again, 'Go to Brimscombe Port Amos, go to Brimscombe Port.' This time he lit the candle beside the bed, checked his wife was asleep (she was) and then got up and looked under the bed, behind the door and even out of the window into the branches of the old apple tree. No one there. *How strange*, he thought, *it must have been a dream*. And he went back to sleep.

Well he heard that voice again the next night and the one after that and the one after that. On and on for a week, for two weeks, for a month and always saying the same thing, 'Go to Brimscombe Port Amos, go to Brimscombe Port.' In the end, Amos thought to himself, *Dreams are dreams, who knows what they are for, perhaps I ought to listen to this one.*

Now, by this time, all the family knew about his voice in the night but, even so, they were surprised when he announced one morning, 'I'm off to Brimscombe Port, I'll only be away a day or two. I have a feeling this dream is trying to tell me something. John will be lock-keeper while I'm gone and you mind you do it well son.'

John beamed with delight and was full of pride – he would show his father and all the boat people just what a good lock-keeper he could be.

Well, the first boat that came through the lock going east that day was a narrowboat called the *Mary Rose* with a load of coal for the Stroud mills. The cargo filled the hold and there wasn't an inch of spare room aboard. Amos asked the skipper if he could take him to Brimscombe.

'Sorry Amos, we've no space and the extra weight would slow us up … the donkeys are tired enough as it is.'

Amos understood; time was important to the boatmen and if anything slowed them up they could lose money and trade.

Half an hour later a fine strong trow approached the lock. Although she was a sailing ship, sails were difficult to use on the canal, and trows weren't allowed through the locks with their sails up, so she was being pulled by a horse who strained on the rope that connected him with the mast. Amos could see the trow's name, *Barbara of Gloster*, painted along the side. He knew this trow well and the skipper. It was laden with wood, brought down from Gloucester and bound for Wallbridge and then on, along the Thames and Severn canal to Brimscombe Port, where all the cargo would be taken off and loaded onto a narrowboat or a barge that could take it to Cirencester.

The skipper was surprised when Amos shouted out. 'Have you got room for one, can I travel with you to Brimscombe? I've a bit of business there.' He had never seen Amos anywhere else – only up and down the locks he looked after – but he replied, 'Yes, I've a young lad that I'm training up on board but if you'll give us a hand along the way and help unload, I'll take you.'

So Amos climbed aboard. He waved goodbye to Mary, John, Charlotte, Martha – and Tan the dog, who ran along the towpath barking anxiously because his master had never gone off without him before.

It was a beautiful late spring morning and his apple tree was covered in white frothy blossom – he watched it disappear behind him and then turned his attention to the canal ahead. Sunlight glinted on the water, ducks with ducklings and moorhens with their young scurried through the water, he heard the splash of an otter and saw a heron standing still as a statue on the bank. He hardly ever left his stretch of the canal because there was always work to be done, week in, week out, and this expedition to Brimscombe Port felt like an adventure.

The skipper was gruff now they were under way; he didn't say much but Amos made himself useful. For a while he walked along the towpath, encouraging the horse, keeping just behind him. This meant the lad could stay onboard and learn more about handling the trow. A long tow rope ran from the bow to the horse's harness and the strong animal hauled the heavy boat along. At midday, Amos was told to fill the horse's nosebag with oats so that he could feed as he trudged the towpath and keep his strength up. A narrowboat travelling west, and pulled by two mules, or 'hanimals' as they were called, passed them and, at a sign from the skipper, Amos slowed the horse so that his rope sank down in the water and the narrowboat was able to glide over the top of it.

The men on board shouted a rough 'Thanks' and then added, 'The locks are for you.'

When they got to the next lock – Dudbridge – the gates were open and waiting; it was Amos and the lad who closed them once the *Barbara of Gloster* was inside. Then Amos took the windlass and opened the sluices in the far gates to raise the water level. He liked this change from his normal work and he was eager to get to Brimscombe Port and find out what his dream meant.

And so the day passed well enough.

It was late afternoon when they finally got to Brimscombe Port and it was bustling. This was an important place where the broad Thames and Severn canal coming from Stroud narrowed. There was a large island in the centre with a lockable swing bridge so that valuable cargoes could be stored for a short time on the island, safe from thieves and pilferers. Just beyond the port there was a boat-building yard with dry docks where both trows and narrow boats were built.

Everywhere Amos looked men were busy loading and unloading cargoes – grain, salt, hops, cider, timber, hides and coal. The canal barges coming down the Thames and Severn couldn't travel beyond Brimscombe because the locks were too short and the trows coming up from Stroud couldn't travel any further because the locks were too narrow, so all their goods had to be unloaded from one type of boat and loaded onto another at this hectic meeting point.

Amos helped to unload the timber and then, weary to the bone, he wrapped himself in a blanket and slept on the deck that night under the stars. The next morning he wondered where he should go and what he should do to find out why the dream had led him to Brimscombe Port. In the end he crossed over the swing bridge to the island and stood there looking about. He watched and waited and waited and watched. Nothing happened. The day was bright and sunny and, although it was a pleasant change for Amos to be doing nothing much, he felt awkward and a little foolish. A few men stared at him but most took no notice and, when evening came, he left the island and walked over to the Ship Inn.

I s'pose this has all been a waste of time and tomorrow I'd best get on home, he thought sadly to himself.

As soon as he'd got his beer and sat down in a corner, an old man he had never seen before – not a local either by the look of him and his strange clothes – came and sat opposite him.

'Whatever are you doing friend? I'm not from these parts, not a boat man myself, but I've been watching you all day, standing on the island doing nothing, gazing about as idle as anything, and now you're sitting here looking like a lost soul. What's it all about?'

Amos was glad to have someone to talk to. 'Well you see it's like this ... I had a dream ...'

'You had a dream! Don't talk to me about dreams, dreams well ... last night I had a dream myself ... dreamt I was somewhere further off ... it was called Ryeford I think and I was outside a brick cottage and there was a beautiful apple tree in full blossom and the canal just in front of it. And what I was doing was digging under this apple tree and do you know what ... there down in the roots, there was a chest of gold. Well if you think I'm going to travel up and down the canals just because of a dream, you'd better think aga–'

He stopped mid-sentence because Amos had gone. He had leapt to his feet and was running as fast as ever he could. And he didn't stop running for nigh on three hours. He ran past the locks whose names he knew so well – Gough's Orchard, Ham Mill, Griffins, Bowbridge, Wallbridge, Dudbridge – until at last, late at night, he came to Ryeford Double Lock.

Tan, his tail wagging furiously, came running down the towpath to meet him. 'Ssshh boy – don't wake everyone,' Amos said, patting the dog's head – but even then he didn't stop. Mary, John and the girls were in bed by the time he got home but he just ran round to the shed, got his shovel and, by the light of the full moon, he began to dig under the apple tree.

It wasn't long before the blade of his shovel struck something hard. He put it down and scrabbled with his hands in the dark earth until he uncovered the edge of a small metal chest. Slowly, he prised it from the roots of the tree, opened it with his heart pounding and found that it was full of gold coins.

Amos was a rich man. He was able to buy the cottage his parents rented so that they could live there securely all the rest of their days. He was able to provide well for his family but he stayed on as a lock-keeper – that was the life he loved – and whenever he chatted to the boats coming through he would say, 'You can never tell what's coming, so follow your dreams ... there may be treasure in them.'

NOTES

Amos is a fictional character. A certain William Hairs was probably the lock-keeper at Ryeford Double Lock in 1836. The double lock at Ryeford, with two locks sharing a middle gate, is the only one of its kind on the Cotswold canals.

Amos lived and worked on the Stroudwater Canal, which ran then, as it does now, from Framilode on the River Severn to Stroud. On his journey from Ryeford Double Lock to Brimscombe Port he would have passed through Wallbridge, Stroud, where the Stroudwater ends and the Thames and Severn canal begins.

Among his many tasks, Amos greased the paddle gear on the lock gates. This is the mechanism that opens and shuts the sluice or paddle that controls the water flow.

The *Barbara of Gloster* on which Amos travelled was a Severn trow (rhymes with crow) probably built of oak from the Forest of Dean. These magnificent ships first sailed the estuary in the fifteenth century and could be seen in the Stroud valley as late as the First World War. They were flat-bottomed because they needed to negotiate the Severn's shallows and sandbanks, and their skippers were skilled in navigating the difficulties and dangers of the estuary. Nevertheless, these treacherous waters still claimed many trows and their crews over the centuries. This story is set in the heyday of the Severn trows when inland and estuary trade was plentiful and the railway had not yet arrived. For the timber on the *Barbara* to reach Cirencester it would have to be transported along a short canal that branched off the Thames and Severn at Siddington.

When this trow was not under sail, she was pulled along the canal by a horse – something that had only been possible since 1825 on the Stroudwater Canal. Before that, there was no towpath as such and men with ropes had to bowhaul the trows while struggling and straining along muddy field edges and over stiles. A horse on the towpath could do the work of several bowhauling men.

The Company of Proprietors from whom Amos rented his cottage was set up in the 1730s and still exists. It is thought to be the oldest surviving canal company in the world. Nowadays, the Company is run by a team of voluntary directors who ensure that the Stroudwater Navigation is managed for the benefit of the people of Stroud as detailed in the most recent Act of 1954. Currently they are working in partnership with the Cotswold Canals Trust, Gloucestershire County Council and Stroud District Council to ensure the full restoration of the Stroudwater Navigation.

Amos' anxieties about his parents and his fear that they might end up in the workhouse would have been very real concerns for a poor family in the 1830s. A new union workhouse had just been built beside the canal at Eastington where inmates were clothed and fed in return for several hours' work each day – often picking oakum or breaking stones. Conditions were deliberately harsh, so that only those who desperately needed help would ask for it. Elderly couples would be split up and housed in different parts of the workhouse.

The narrowboat *Mary Rose,* which was too heavily laden to give Amos a lift, was carrying a load of coal to the Stroud mills. The mills were famous for fine quality woollen broadcloth and, to produce this, they needed several thousand tons of coal a year. The boat was pulled by donkeys. It is said that donkeys (which could pull heavy barges but not ploughs) were often used instead of horses because local farmers and others were less likely to steal them.

The Ship Inn at Brimscombe Port is still there today – you may wish to buy a beer and sit down in the corner just as Amos did – although I cannot guarantee that a stranger will appear and interpret your dreams.

5

KATE THE BOAT-BUILDER'S DAUGHTER, 1854

LAUNCHING A TROW

Kate snuggled down under the blankets for her bedtime story. She could hear the wind blowing down the canal outside the cottage and hear the water gently gurgling past. An owl hooted and, inside, the candle beside her bed flickered sending shadows across the ceiling, as her mother began.

'Well, I am going to tell you a story that was a favourite of mine when I was your age ...

'There was once a King who had three daughters and he decided to ask each of them how much they loved him. "As much as life," said the first. "Better than all the world," said the second. The King was pleased. "I love you as meat loves salt," said the third. This made the King angry. "You don't love me at all," he shouted and he drove her out of the house, shutting the door behind her. The poor girl wandered away until she came to a fen.'

'What's a fen?' asked Kate.

'A watery place.'

Ah, thought Kate. *Like here.*

'She came to the fen and gathered rushes and made herself a cloak with a hood to hide her fine clothes. Then she wandered on until she came to a large house and there she begged for a job and was set to work scrubbing pans in the kitchen. She told no one her name and they called her Cap o' Rushes.

'One day there was to be a great dance nearby and all the servants were going along to look at the grand people. Cap o' Rushes said she was tired and would stay at home but, when they had gone, she took off her cloak and washed and went to the dance. Well, the master's son was there and he fell in love with her and would not dance with anyone else. But, before the evening was over, Cap o' Rushes left and went home. When the others returned they told her of the beautiful, mysterious lady and said, "You must come tonight, there is to be another dance."'

'Did she go?' asked Kate.

'Yes, she went that night and the one after but each time she arrived after everyone else and left before the dance was over.

'On the third night, the master's son asked her who she was but Cap o' Rushes wouldn't say. Then he gave her a ring and said if he did not see her again he would die. Over the next few days, he tried every way he knew to find out who this lady was. But nobody could tell him and the master's son grew weaker and sadder until he took to his bed.

'Now it's time to go to sleep,' said her mother.

'Oh, tell me the rest of the story,' begged Kate.

'No, not now, it's late and we've got a busy exciting day tomorrow. Go to sleep, and when you wake up it will be your birthday.'

Her mother blew out the candle and Kate turned over and was soon fast asleep.

When she awoke next morning – 8 February 1854 – the minute Kate opened her eyes, she was excited. It was her seventh birthday and she knew a treat was planned – though no one would tell her what it was. She looked out of the window and saw the blue flash of a kingfisher across the canal and then a couple of donkeys plodded by in harnesses hauling a barge of coal up the canal from Stroud.

Kate ran down the stairs of the small canalside cottage near Brimscombe where she lived. Her father, Stephen Holdman, had already gone to work but her mother was filling the kettle for some tea.

'It's today isn't it? What are we doing? Where are we going?'

'It is Kate, today you are 7, happy birthday. Now get dressed and eat some breakfast and then we can set off.'

'Yes but where? Are we going to see one of father's boats?'

'It's a secret.'

Kate was pretty sure they were going to the Bourne – the small boat-building docks where her father worked, just the other side of Brimscombe Port from where they lived. Boats, barges and trows had been part of Kate's life as long as she could remember. Her father and his team of skilled carpenters built sturdy, flat-bottomed Stroud barges out of oak and elm – he always came home smelling of tar and sawdust.

Sometimes Kate and her mother would go and meet him at the end of the day and he would show her the boat they were working on. Her father was proud of his skills and how the team built boats by eye with no drawings or machines.

'Where will this one go, what will it carry?' Kate always asked.

'Well, my girl,' her father would reply, 'it'll maybe take cloth from the Stroud mills to Bristol and then no doubt they'll be coal to bring back from across the Severn at Lydney or even timber from the Forest of Dean.'

Anyway, this particular morning, Kate dressed, ate her breakfast of bread, butter and tea, and then put on her lace-up boots ready to set off up the towpath towards

Brimscombe Port. She was looking forward to watching the boats go through Bourne Lock – 'our special lock', her father called it – the only one of its kind on the whole canal big enough to take both the wide sailing trows and the long barges. But, to her surprise, her mother turned and walked the other way towards Stroud.

'Where are we going?'

'Wait and see. It's a surprise.'

Kate skipped about with excitement, which grew as they met more and more people walking the same way – many dressed in their best clothes and all in a good mood. There were so many on the towpath that when they met a horse coming the other way – hauling a trow laden with grain – they had to squash up to let it past and it was a wonder no one slipped and fell into the canal. Kate and her mother were pushed towards the rushes at the edge of the path.

'I wish I had a Cap o' Rushes,' said Kate. 'Will you tell me the rest of the story?'

'We're nearly there,' said her mother. 'I'll tell you the rest of the story when we get home. Now look ahead.'

They were surrounded by people laughing and chatting, and Kate still had no idea where they were going. Then, when they came round the corner and saw Wallbridge just up ahead, she understood what all the fuss was about. There in the wharf, ready to be launched, was a magnificent trow – a type of sailing ship that worked on the Stroudwater Navigation and the River Severn in those days. Her wooden sides were gleaming and her name *Longney* was proudly painted around the bow.

Crowds of people lined the canal banks on either side and, as she got nearer, Kate could see that *Longney* was sitting on greased rollers that ran across the towpath. They came to a halt quite near to these rollers. The crowd was very excited … something was about to happen. Kate realised they were just in time as one man – Captain Longney after whom the trow was named – gave a shout of command and several strong men began to shove and push the *Longney* over the rollers until, with an enormous splash, she toppled into the canal and then came to rest upright, sitting proudly in the water. Everyone on the bank opposite was soaked and, as they gasped and spluttered with the shock of it, the crowd around Kate laughed. Then a huge cheer went up and a shout of *Longney*!

Men on the bank had kept hold of strong ropes and now pulled the trow into the side, a gangplank was laid from the bank to the trow and the skipper went on board and raised the mast. More cheers!

Mr John Biddle, the trow's owner and a miller from Stratford Mills, was the first dignitary on board, followed by Captain Longney and many important looking men, who went to the decks at either end of the trow. Then the entire Ebley brass band filled the hold. Several speeches were made before the *Longney* set off down the canal towards Dudbridge pulled by a strong, brown horse, its coat gleaming and its mane plaited with ribbons. A long rope ran from the mast to the horse's harness. Suddenly there was a huge bang as a cannon fired a celebratory salute from Rodborough Fort, the horse was startled and had to be quieted and, just as it settled down, there was more commotion as the brass band struck up 'Life on the Ocean Wave'. All along the bank Kate could see people waving and cheering. It was the most exciting birthday she had ever had.

With her mother and most of the crowd, Kate walked along the muddy towpath following the progress of the *Longney*. The winter sun was shining and they were singing along with the band and admiring this fine boat with its Union Jack fluttering in the wind. At Dudbridge, beer and lemonade were served, the band played lively waltzes and some of the crowd danced while others clapped. It was mid-afternoon by the time they set off home.

'Make sure you remember everything,' said her mother, 'so that we can tell your father what we've seen.'

That night as her mother prepared a stew of vegetables and a bit of bacon, Kate washed the pans and imagined herself as Cap o' Rushes in the kitchen of a grand house. While they worked, her mother told her the rest of the story.

'The cook was ordered to make a broth for the master's son who was dying for love of the lady but Cap o' Rushes said, "Let me make it." She slipped the ring into the broth and when the young man found it at the bottom of the bowl he was amazed and sent for the cook. She could not explain it and was frightened to tell the master's son that it was not her who had made the broth. "Tell me who it was," he said. "You will not be harmed."

'So it was that Cap o' Rushes was sent for and when the truth came out and she revealed who she was, the master's son got well very soon and a grand wedding was planned. Everyone was invited from far and near, including Cap o' Rushes' father. But before the wedding she went to the cook and said not even a grain of salt was to be used in any dish. The cook reluctantly agreed but only because Cap o' Rushes was now an important lady. *It will all be tasteless*, the poor cook thought.

'When the wedding feast was served all the guests struggled to eat the food that tasted so bland. Cap o' Rushes' father tried one dish and then another, and then tears began to trickle down his face.

'"What is the matter," said the master's son.

'"I once had a daughter who told me she loved me as much as meat loves salt. I turned her from my door because I thought she did not love me and now I see she loved me best of all. And, for all I know, she may now be dead."

'"No father here she is," said Cap o' Rushes, and they put their arms around each other and laughed and wept and there was great rejoicing. And, of course, they all lived happily ever after.'

'I like that story,' said Kate.

After supper, the family sat round the fire and Kate told her father about her wonderful day. She giggled when she described the wave that soaked the people on the bank. Then her father produced from his jacket pocket something wrapped in brown paper.

'A present for your birthday.'

It was a model of a Stroud barge with a cargo of salt. Kate looked at her mother and they both laughed.

'Thank you,' she said, hugging her father. 'I love it and I love you as much as meat loves salt.'

NOTES

Kate lived near Brimscombe Port on the Thames and Severn canal. Beyond the port itself, just before the canal narrows, you can still see Bourne Lock, which was indeed the only lock on the Cotswold canals large enough to take both trows and long barges.

The other side of Bourne Lock was the Bourne yard where her father worked. A boat-builder's yard with two dry docks that have now been filled in, it was the major yard of its kind on the two canals. A variety of boats, including Stroud barges, were built and repaired here and, on her visits to see her father at work, Kate would no doubt have relished watching the boats reach the canal from the dry docks. The large dock gates, hinged at the bottom, would be dropped flat onto the canal bed so that the newly built boat could simply float out.

The first two barges to be built at the Bourne – aptly named the *Severn* and the *Thames* – were launched in 1786 and the yard's boat-building designs became so good

that by the 1790s they were being copied by boat-builders on the Thames. Much of the oak and elm required to build the boats would have come from the Forest of Dean. There were nearby yards at Stroud, Chalford and Framilode but the Bourne, at this period, was the most productive. The skilled workers seldom used drawings or even models and often set up the frames of the boats by eye alone.

Flat-bottomed Stroud barges, with their sharp bows and sterns, were built at the Bourne and were primarily designed to bring coal from Bullo Pill in the Forest of Dean to Brimscombe and beyond. Boat-building continued at the Bourne until well into the twentieth century.

Kate's father gave her a model of a barge used for carrying salt, and this cargo would have been brought from Droitwich via the Severn and then the Gloucester and Sharpness canal onto the Stroudwater Navigation and then the Thames and Severn. A salt warehouse can still be seen at Brimscombe Port today.

Joan Tucker, in her book *The Stroudwater Navigation,* describes the spectacular launch of the *Longney* at Wallbridge on 8 February 1854 with all the celebrations and festivities mentioned.

6

JIM THE BARGE-MASTER'S SON, 1870

TRANSPORTING A CARGO DOWN TO THE THAMES

Not so very long ago (150 years or so) and not so very far away – down the valley east towards the Thames – there lived a bargemaster, his wife and their son, Jim. They lived in Chalford and their home was at Chalford Wharf. The father made a good living from his fleet of barges, trows (on the Stroudwater canal) and narrowboats.

He bought and sold coal from Cardiff, willow from Wiltshire, stone from Chepstow and iron from Gloucester, and he delivered all these goods to wharves along the Stroud valley and up into the Cotswolds. All along the canals, in both directions, his boats would travel with their various cargoes. They took hay from Stroud to London, wood from Woodchester to the Black Country, slate and cement from Gloucester to Birmingham and sawdust from Ryeford to the bacon curers of Cirencester!

Most impressive of all was the timber from the huge redwood trees of Archangel that his barges carried on the last leg of its journey from Russia to Reading.

Now Jim, well he was a dreamer and everyone, even his father, thought he was lazy. The other young men teased and bullied him, and Jim tried to stay out of their way. What he liked to do best was to wander along the canal with his tin, sit down at his favourite spot, opposite the Chalford roundhouse, and watch the world go by. Sometimes he would shout out greetings or a bit of chat to the men on the boats as they went by.

One morning a smart, newly painted longboat, the *Rosemary*, approached – Jim knew her and her owner by sight. She was pulled by a sturdy brown horse, her cargo was covered over and a young boy was moving nervously about, obviously on his first trip. Jim shouted to the skipper, 'Where are you bound?'

'Coates today Jim and then on through the tunnel all the way to Inglesham.'

'What's your cargo?'

'The best timber – brought it up from Gloucester bound for the Thames.'

When the boat had gone on, Jim settled down to have his lunch. He took out the tin he always carried

everywhere – often with a bit of bread and cheese in it. It was no ordinary tin, well not to Jim anyway. Beautifully decorated, it had the royal crest in the middle of the lid surrounded by intricate oriental designs of red and yellow and blue and black. A boatman he had once helped through the locks had given it to him years before; Jim had no idea where it had come from but it was now his most treasured possession.

He had just taken the first mouthful, and was sitting there dangling his feet in the canal, when two local lads crept up behind him, pounced on the tin and started to throw it wildly from one to another. Jim jumped up and tried to catch it but one particularly vicious throw sent the tin spinning into the canal. The lads ran off laughing. Jim was furious and upset, but by the time several boats had passed and he could wade into the canal there was no sign of the tin.

When he told his father, the bargemaster said it was time he grew up and stopped worrying about an old tin.

'I'm going to send you on a boat up to Coates with a load of coal and see if we can't make a man of you.'

And so it was that Jim was given an old canal boat, battered and bashed with its paintwork all peeling, an old man with stiff joints and poor eyesight to help him, a worn out pair of donkeys, long past work, and a cargo of slack. He didn't mind, he was pleased to have his own boat and to be going off into the world.

Jim enjoyed the challenge, and he worked harder than he had ever done in his life. He and the old man got along well – Jim took charge of the donkeys, all the work of getting through the locks and hiring leggers to move the boat through the long, dark tunnel at Sapperton. The old man steered and made the tea.

When they reached Coates on the other side of the tunnel, Jim was surprised to see the *Rosemary* moored up and he tied up his boat behind. The skipper was nowhere to be seen and the young boy Jim had seen on board back at Chalford was hanging around looking as nervous as ever.

'Where's your skipper?' asked Jim

'Taken ill, he's bad with fever. His sister's sent a cart and horse to fetch him. I'm in charge and I don't know as I can do it – get this cargo of timber to Inglesham you know. Not on my own like.'

He looked sad and worried but Jim's ears pricked up.

'I could do it with your help. What do you say we work the *Rosemary* together? I'll sell my cargo of coal and that will pay for the old man to travel back to Chalford. Then I can find grazing for the donkeys and leave my boat here. We can set off on an adventure of our own.'

And so it was. Jim and the lad, Billy, left word of their plans at the inn and set off next morning in late spring sunshine. The banks were full of water buttercups and bullrushes, ducks with their young in tow paddled in the canal and everything was fresh and exciting. The two young men travelled over the next week through Siddington and Cerney Wick to Marston Meysey, on to Kempsford and finally towards Inglesham, where the canal met the Thames.

As they were approaching Inglesham, Jim saw, amidst the willow trees, a stone roundhouse very similar to the one he used to sit opposite in Chalford and he thought about home and his parents and wondered how they were getting on. He wasn't making lots of money as they might wish but he was having a wonderful time.

Just then, out of the corner of his eye, Jim suddenly saw a little child – 2 or 3 years old perhaps – run across the towpath chasing a kitten but then stumble and, to Jim's horror, fall with a splash into the canal. A young woman appeared from the roundhouse, saw the splash and cried out. She was just about to wade into the water in her long skirt but Jim got there first. He slid over the side of the boat – the water was only up to his thighs – and waded to where the little boy was spluttering, crying and flailing his arms around. Heaving the child, who was soaked, upset but not hurt, up onto his shoulders, Jim made his way to the bank and gave him to the young woman.

'Oh thank you, thank you. I don't know what's to be done with Ned. He runs off every time my back is turned. I only went to feed the hens and when I come back he's in the canal. But you pulled him out with no harm done.' She laughed with relief.

'I'm Sarah, I'm the lengthsman's daughter and Ned is my little brother. We live here. Come in, come in, I'm sure my father would like to thank you.'

So Jim and Billy were taken into the roundhouse to meet Sarah's parents and, while she changed Ned into some dry clothes, they thanked him profusely.

'I've been the lengthsman here for thirty years and I've seen many fall in the canal but never one of my own family. Now tell me young man, where are you going with that cargo of timber?

'Well to be truthful, sir, I'm not sure,' and Jim explained about the skipper who was ill and had gone to stay with his sister and how the cargo belonged to the skipper really not him or Billy.

'Why don't you write to him, tell him you're at Inglesham roundhouse and while you're waiting for a reply stay here both of you as our guests.'

And that's what they did. Billy had the address of the skipper's sister and so they wrote him a letter saying the timber had been safely transported as far as Inglesham and they were awaiting his orders.

Jim loved the few days that followed. In the mornings he would go out with Sarah's father and help him keep the towpath clear, cutting back brambles, filling the punt with prunings and inspecting the stonework. Sometimes they would have a shouting chat with the men passing in their boats just as Jim used to do in Chalford. In the evenings, after sharing a meal with all the family, Jim and Sarah – who were becoming very fond of one another – would walk beside the canal chatting and telling one another about their lives, their families and their dreams.

One day, about a week after Ned fell in the canal, the postman delivered a letter from the skipper. He was full of praise for what they had done and enclosed some money for their work. He was still ill but getting better and he said if they were happy to take the timber on to Reading and sell it there, the money would be theirs and he looked forward to seeing them and the boat on their return.

Well, Billy was eager to get home, he didn't want to go on to Reading. Jim tried to think what to do but all he could really think about was Sarah and how much he wanted to stay with her. That evening on their walk, he told her how he felt and she said she had loved him from the moment he rescued little Ned. Suddenly, Jim knew what to do and, falling onto one knee on the muddy towpath, he asked Sarah to marry him. She beamed with pleasure and agreed and, in quiet delight, they began to plan a life together on the canals. Her family were very pleased and a quiet wedding was held two days later. Billy got a ride on a boat going back down the canal to Chalford and Jim and Sarah set off together along the Thames to Reading with their cargo of timber.

It was hard and sometimes dangerous work navigating the river and its currents in their flat-bottomed boat and the journey to Reading was a long one. Jim was further away from home than he had ever been in his life.

One morning he awoke to a sweet, mouth-watering smell in the air and asked Sarah what it was.

'Oh that's the biscuit factory you can smell. Best biscuits in the whole world come from Reading!'

Jim was intrigued and when eventually they reached the wharf and sold their cargo for a good price, he and Sarah followed their noses and set off into the town. Soon enough they came to an enormous biscuit factory with carts lined up outside onto which brightly decorated tins of every size and description were being stacked – each one with a different selection of biscuits inside. Although the smell was tantalising, it wasn't that which held Jim's attention – it was something else entirely. Something beautifully decorated and reassuringly familiar ... a tin with the royal crest in the middle of the lid surrounded by intricate oriental designs of red and yellow and blue and black.

This was where his beautiful tin came from ... and now he had found another – well hundreds of others.

Jim spoke to a distinguished-looking older man who had just come out of the factory and he asked him breathlessly how he could buy one of these tins.

'Where are you from, young man, you're obviously not from round here?'

'No, sir, I've come from Chalford down the canal to Inglesham ... but I once had one of your tins ...'
and, as he told the whole story, the older man listened with great interest.

'Well Jim I own this factory and I reckon providence sent you to me. You see I have been wanting to send my biscuits to the Cotswolds and I have been planning to find a carrier who would take them there. Perhaps you are just the man.'

And to Jim's astonishment, he and Sarah were invited into the owner's office and given tea and the most delicious biscuits they had ever tasted. They found themselves agreeing to take 500 boxes of the best biscuits up the Thames and Severn canal. They could sell them along the way and, if all went well, there would be plenty more trade in the future. The newly married couple were delighted – here was work that might well keep them busy and well paid for a long time to come.

So the boat was loaded with tins of biscuits and they set off. The first thing Jim did was put aside one for himself – he would share the biscuits with Sarah but the tin would be his ... his bread and cheese box to replace the one he had treasured.

Many weeks later, after a wonderful journey back along the Thames and then down the canal, Jim and Sarah reached Chalford. At every town, village and tiny settlement they had passed through the local people had been keen to buy the tins of biscuits and so now they had money in their pockets. Jim's father and mother were amazed at all their son had achieved and welcomed his lovely wife with open arms. As for the local lads, well they were probably jealous of Jim's new-found wealth and his beautiful bride but no one ever, ever teased Jim nor called him lazy again.

NOTES

The roundhouse at Chalford where Jim sits at the beginning of the story, and that at Inglesham where Sarah lives, both still exist. They are two of five such roundhouses, built as lengthsmen's cottages, along the

29-mile Thames and Severn canal. The ground floor would have been used for stabling and the upper floors for living accommodation.

Jim and Billy travel up the Thames and Severn, which was completed in 1789 and ran from Wallbridge near Stroud, where it connected with the Stroudwater Navigation, to the river Thames at Inglesham Lock near Lechlade. A tributary canal ran from the Thames and Severn at Siddington to Cirencester.

Although there were problems with leaks and shortages of water from the very beginning, the canal continued in use until the early twentieth century.

Lengthsmen like Sarah's father worked on the canals and were particularly responsible for lengths of towpath and, in the absence of a lock-keeper, for locks and their trappings and surroundings. Their duties included the management of water levels and the control of weirs. Lengthsmen were also responsible for repair and maintenance of banks on their 'length', including cutting reeds and vegetation and the treading of puddle clay into sections of bank that were weak or suffering from leakage.

The biscuit factory that Jim and Sarah come across is based loosely on the renowned company Huntley & Palmers which had its headquarters in Reading and became, in its time, the world's largest biscuit manufacturer. Their wares were preserved in locally produced and elaborately decorated biscuit tins, which proved to be a highly successful marketing tool and became collectors' items. The company did use the Kennet and Avon canal to transport their biscuits to Bristol and Bath, although there is no evidence for similar trade on the Thames and Severn Canal. Huntley & Palmers would have preferred the canal route to the roads since it was much cheaper and there was less risk of damage from vibration. However, it would soon prove very slow compared to the new railways.

7

ELIZABETH THE SWIMMER, 1930s

TAKING PART IN THE WALLBRIDGE GALA

Elizabeth was born in Cainscross in the 1920s and, from a very young age, the Stroudwater Navigation was to her a rather special place.

As a toddler, Elizabeth would wait eagerly for her father's return from work. As soon as he walked through the door, he would give her and her older brother Bertie a big hug and they would set off on their daily walk down to the canal and along the towpath – Bertie on foot and Elizabeth on her father's shoulders.

From her vantage point, Elizabeth would sit up proud like a princess and survey her domain. The tree-lined canal, its water sometimes dark and murky, sometimes sparkling in the evening sunshine, the dusty towpath edged with hawthorn and blackberries, the bullrushes and marsh marigolds that flowered beside the water itself. Some evenings she spotted water voles, occasionally a kingfisher and, if she was really lucky, an otter swimming sleek and strong through the water. Elizabeth wanted to swim like that.

On one such walk, on a dappled summer evening, when Elizabeth was about 3 years old, she was silently enjoying their ramble, sitting up high as usual and listening to her brother's chatter and her father's measured replies. Unexpectedly, she heard a gentle splash behind her and, holding on to her father's ears, Elizabeth swivelled her head to see what had caused it. To her delight an otter had poked its head out of the water and was looking straight at her with its bright, dark eyes. It looked friendly and interested in her and Elizabeth stared back hoping it would stay there for just a little while. However, before she even had time to pull on her father's ears and make him look, the otter had dived gracefully into the canal and disappeared, leaving only ripples on the surface. From then on Elizabeth eagerly scanned the water on every walk hoping that somehow she would see 'her otter' again and she talked incessantly about wanting to dive and swim in the canal.

By the time she started school, Elizabeth was well aware of the groups of older children who gathered on the canal banks in the late afternoon to swim and jump and play around in the water and she longed to join them. She had seen some of the braver ones diving off Hilly Orchard bridge and thought it the most exciting thing in the world.

'Let me swim, I want to dive,' she would say pleadingly to her father on their evening walks.

'Not yet Lizzie, maybe when you're a bit older,' was the disappointing reply.

Elizabeth's mother had been a keen swimmer when she was a girl and, pleased at her daughter's enthusiasm, she promised to take her to the Stroud Swimming Club's annual swimming gala at Wallbridge in Stroud. This was a major event in the local calendar and every July competitors from all over the locality would gather to show their skills at plunging, diving, swimming and water polo. Elizabeth was thrilled, especially at the prospect of seeing the school relay races.

If she was excited before the event, Elizabeth's enthusiasm knew no bounds on the day itself. She jumped up and down with excitement as they waited for the bus, pulled at her mother's hand to get them there as fast as possible and, when they got to the upper basin at Wallbridge and joined the spectators on the wharf, she was beside herself with eager anticipation.

Everywhere there were groups of swimmers with towels around their shoulders, waiting their turn, chatting to each other or eyeing up the competitors. The water looked cool and clear and there was a plank strung across the canal on which those in the next event lined up ready to start.

'Who is that? What are they going to do?' Elizabeth asked, pointing to each competitor in turn. Her mother consulted the programme and patiently explained the events and who was taking part. The little girl stared in awe at girls from the local schools who were waiting to swim in the relay race.

When this longed-for event finally arrived, she watched eagerly as the youngsters lined up on the plank, some of them nervously scanning the crowd for those they knew, and then, at the signal, they dived into the water and swam for all they were worth, churning up the usually calm canal as their schoolmates shouted out every sort of encouragement. Then came the naming of the winners and the applause. It was thrilling.

'Did you enjoy today?' her mother asked when it was all over.

'Yes, yes, yes and I want to swim in the relay,' replied Elizabeth.

'Well,' said her mother 'you are very lucky because your school is one of those that takes part in the gala each year and when you are a bit older you can start to practise and I will show you what I know.'

'But I want to swim now,' said Elizabeth, 'please.'

But she had to wait until her parents deemed her old enough to go with Bertie down to the canal, where a group of children spent most summer evenings swimming and shouting, daring and diving. There, at last, Elizabeth was able to start on her long-held ambitions. Holding on to the memories of the relay event she had seen at Wallbridge, she watched the others, copied them, practised until she could swim without touching the bottom and then made Bertie teach her how to dive.

Elizabeth's enthusiasm never waned and she became a very strong and determined swimmer and, when she was 10 years old, the first of her dreams came true.

'Mum, guess what happened at school today,' she said as she burst through the front door, trying to disguise her excitement.

Her mother looked at Elizabeth, held out her arms and smiled.

'You've been picked for the relay team haven't you?'

'Yes, yes, yes,' she said as she was hugged.

'Well I am very proud of you. Well done. We will all be there at Wallbridge cheering you on.'

After that, every spare moment was spent either in the water or practising dives from the bank. Until that is the fateful weekend when Harry came to stay. Harry was their cousin from over Cheltenham way and he often came to stay for the Whitsun weekend. The children got on well and even though Harry was not a swimmer they found plenty of other things to do down at Victory Park or racing each other from bridge to bridge along the towpath.

This year, however, Bertie couldn't wait to show Harry something secret and special that he had been making especially for his cousin's visit. He led Harry and Elizabeth down to the canal to a place where, hidden in the reeds, he proudly pointed to a makeshift raft fashioned out of bits of timber, rope and oil drums. Bertie had built it himself, telling no one, not even his father whom he was sure would want to inspect it. It was to be the children's secret.

'It doesn't matter that you can't swim Harry, we can go along the canal on my raft now,' he said proudly.

If Harry was nervous he didn't show it and with Bertie's help he clambered aboard, Elizabeth close behind him. Bertie pushed them out from the bank with a stout branch he had chosen for the purpose and they began to drift down the canal towards Ebley. For a short while it was thrilling and the children grinned at each other and shouted with glee. Then the trouble started. Unknown to them, one of the oil drums had a series of small holes in it that were letting in water and, as the drum began to fill, the raft tilted to one side and started to sink. Being strong swimmers, Elizabeth and Bertie were not too concerned but when Harry realised what was happening he started frantically shouting that he couldn't swim. Elizabeth saw his terrified face as the raft sunk under them; she caught the flailing boy and tried to pull him towards the bank. Harry struggled, pulling her under so that both of them swallowed great mouthfuls of water and she caught his fear and panic. For the first time in her life, Elizabeth felt frightened in the water. With Bertie's help, she did manage to get her cousin to safety and all was well, but the children were shocked and shaken.

The next evening when Elizabeth went down to the canal to get on with her practice she found to her dismay that she could not bear to put her head under the water. Every time she tried, she would shake and splutter and end up staggering to the bank unable to continue. She did not dare to tell her parents what had happened when Harry was with them and so she could not tell them that she was now, inexplicably, unable to swim. The day of the gala drew near and Elizabeth felt anxious and ashamed. Her mother, her father and her brother – to say nothing of her school friends – would all be there to watch and she would not even be able to start the race, let alone help her school win the cup.

Tired and worried, unable to swim, she nevertheless went for a walk along the towpath the evening before the gala.

It was a dappled summer evening and as she tried to puzzle out what she was going to do, Elizabeth heard a gentle splash behind her. She swivelled her head to see what had caused it and that is when she saw the otter. As Elizabeth stared, the sleek, brown creature seemed to look right at her with its bright, dark eyes and then it dived gracefully into the canal. This time, instead of disappearing, the otter surfaced a little way off and then dived again and again as if inviting Elizabeth to join her. Without even thinking, Elizabeth waded in and found herself swimming in the creature's wake with strong and confident strokes. When she put her head under the water to do a glide she was amazed and delighted to find that the fear had completely gone and her old confidence had returned. When she surfaced, the otter had vanished.

'Thank you, thank you,' the girl whispered to the ripples on the surface.

The Saturday of the gala itself dawned bright and sunny. Elizabeth knew, the moment she opened her eyes, that it was going to be a great day and she had nothing to worry about.

The atmosphere at Wallbridge was one of excitement and celebration. Elizabeth took her place among her school team tense with excitement. When, finally, it was time for the relay event, she strode out into the middle of the plank, smiled at the other competitors, waved at her family and then, as soon as the signal was given, she dived gracefully into the canal, glided streamlined through the water and then swam with every ounce of strength and skill she could muster. Elizabeth knew she was travelling through the water faster than she had ever done before and sure enough, when she handed over the baton, there was an enormous cheer from the crowd – enough to tell her that her team were now certain to win. And they did! Everyone congratulated her and said she was an amazing swimmer. Elizabeth gazed into the crowd, where her father, mother and Bertie were grinning and waving wildly at her in their delight.

The races were followed by a hilarious obstacle race and an even more ridiculous greasy pole competition.

'Look, look,' Elizabeth said between giggles as she pointed to yet another competitor inelegantly tumbling off the pole and hitting the water with a loud splash.

After all the events, a striking young woman came forward to address the crowd. A well-known champion in her own right and much admired by the spectators, this famous athlete announced that, before awarding the cups and certificates, she would be giving a display of diving and the techniques of front crawl. The crowd cheered and Elizabeth watched intently. The perfectly executed dives into the deep water of the lock were so graceful and poised, they made her think of 'her otter'.

'Thank you,' she whispered.

NOTES

For twenty-five years before the opening of the Stroud Lido in 1937, swimming events were held at Wallbridge canal basin, Stroud. The Annual Gala of the Stroud Swimming Club took place on a Saturday in July and was a very popular event in which both children and adults participated.

In the 1930s many local schools took part in the School Relay Race including Church St, Parliament St, Central, Uplands, Thrupp and Cainscross. One of the highlights would be a demonstration by a well-known swimmer of the day, who would then present the cups and prizes.

In 1935 this honour fell to Miss Cicely Cousens, England's champion for that year, who gave a high diving exhibition. In 1936, it was the turn of Miss Shelagh

Browning, who had herself learned to swim at Wallbridge, although her family later moved to Newport. At the age of 18 she was, for the third year in succession, the open long-distance swimming champion of England as well as having won the national Welsh quarter mile and the breaststroke Welsh national title. Miss Browning gave a comprehensive display to the Wallbridge crowd and introduced them to racing speeds and the exercises that formed part of her daily training.

8

ANNA THE TIME TRAVELLER, 2018

COTSWOLD CANALS IN THE PAST AND THE FUTURE

2018: Anna sat on the steps of the Stroud Subscription Rooms feeling lonely and wretched. She didn't like coming into town and she didn't like shopping, but her friends had made fun of her for so long that she had finally agreed to come with them – even though she had no money to spend – and now she was kicking her heels, waiting for them to finish whatever they were doing, and hating every minute of it.

What she wanted was to be down by the canal, at the quiet, hidden place she knew under the old bridge of crumbling bricks – watching the shimmering blue dragonflies dart across the water, seeing the wild roses in the hedge, the bullrushes by the water and the ducklings making their way through the weed-choked water. The canal was Anna's favourite place – her sanctuary – and it was where she went whenever things were horrible at home, whenever her parents were arguing and shouting and slamming doors and she just wanted to be somewhere quiet. Today her dad had yelled at her that she was no good and she was never going to make anything of her life. Her friends teased her, not always kindly, 'Why do you go down to the grotty old canal? You're weird, why don't you come into town and look around the shops?'

As she sat there, bored, watching the minutes tick by on the clock tower, Anna started to daydream about her place under the bridge. Had it always been there? Would it be there for the rest of her life? She hoped so.

Suddenly she realised that everything had gone quiet. The traffic noise had stopped, in fact the cars and vans that had, just a moment ago, been driving through the middle of Stroud had simply disappeared. There were no people on the pavements and a mist was creeping over the town so that she could hardly see the shops around her – the clothes shop, the dry cleaners, the sports shop, all had almost vanished.

Through the mist, she saw a large, shadowy form approaching and, for a moment, she felt afraid and crouched ready to stand up and run. What on earth was happening? Then the mist cleared and, in front of her,

stood a fine, black horse and on its back a woman dressed in silken robes that shimmered like water. Her white hair fell in waves down her back and, on her head, she wore a garland of wild roses. Her face was kind and her eyes sparkled as she motioned to Anna to get up onto the horse behind her and, without knowing how or why, Anna did as she was bid. As soon as she was seated, the horse set off and the water woman (for that was how Anna thought of her) spoke gently saying, 'Where we are going Anna and what we are going to see will make your heart glad.'

Anna had never been on a horse before and she was excited, a little scared and quite bewildered by what was happening. They rode along roads, then lanes and paths that were not really familiar, although sometimes she half recognised a view or a bend in the road. At last they reached the top of a hill and there, in front of them, were three paths.

One was overgrown with weeds and brambles that almost blocked the way, another looked passable though it twisted and turned and there was litter strewn along it. The third was clear and inviting, a grassy path with wildflowers on either side running straight ahead.

'Anna,' said the water woman, 'this is where the three paths meet – distant past, recent past and future. Choose which you will, though we have time to travel them all.'

Anna chose the dark, overgrown path and the horse began to make its way through the weeds, brambles and thistles and between old trees festooned with ivy. Ahead she could hear all manner of sounds and, soon, the path opened out and they were beside the canal. Anna recognised the old bridge – her special hidden place – but almost everything else was different. Instead of peace and quiet there was bustle and activity. A man was leading a horse along the towpath, encouraging it in a loud voice as the horse munched from the bag of oats around its neck and pulled the long rope that led from the halter back to the barge, laden with a cargo of grain that it was hauling along. The skipper on the barge shouted greetings to another going the opposite way – a barge full of coal that sat low in the water – and yelled at the man beside the horse to let the rope slacken so that the heavier barge could pass. Further along, a trow with a cargo of wood was mooring up to wait its turn in the lock. No weeds choked the canal here, although Anna saw with delight a dragonfly darting across the water and a duckling swimming along beside the bank. There were wild roses in the bank just like those in the water woman's hair.

'When was the canal like this?' Anna asked the water woman and she smiled.

'This Anna is 1835, when the canal was thriving. Tons of precious cargo were brought by boat and trow from the Severn to Stroud every day and many people depended for their living on the Stroudwater Navigation as it was called. Stroud was an important canal town.'

Then she turned the horse around and they rode back up the hill to the place where the three paths met. 'Which would you like to take next Anna?' asked the water woman and Anna pointed to the path that twisted and turned with litter scattered all along it. The horse trotted over rustling crisp packets, bits of rusting old iron, past an abandoned pram and tangles of plastic bags until they emerged once more on the canal bank. There was her bridge of crumbling bricks but the horses, the barges, the trow and even the lock were gone and everything looked forlorn, neglected, forgotten. Weeds and rubbish grew so thick between the rotting banks that it was impossible to see the water at all. A lone dragonfly flashed blue as it alighted on a clump of nettles. In the distance Anna could hear the familiar drone of traffic.

'We must be nearer my time now,' said Anna. 'I can hear cars nearby but it's not quite my own time because when I go to my special place by the bridge, it's much nicer than this mess.'

'Yes,' said the water woman. 'We are now in 1972 – over forty-five years ago – before anyone started work on restoring the canal. You see, after the railways came, the canals gradually stopped being used until eventually no one travelled on them and most people forgot that they were even here. Now in your time, in 2018, they are being brought back to life – many sections have been cleared of choking weeds, the water can flow again, locks have been rebuilt and, on a few short stretches, there are sometimes boats and canoes, but in 1972 this is how it looked.'

'What a lot has been done since then,' said Anna. 'Now can I see the third path, the future?'

And they turned and rode back to where the three paths forked. There was the one they had not yet travelled

– clear and inviting, a grassy path with wildflowers on either side running straight ahead. The horse trotted down it, the scent of the flowers filling their nostrils, and, as they emerged from between two trees onto the canalside, they almost collided with a family of cyclists pedalling along the towpath – mother and father with a toddler in the buggy pod behind. Anna watched them until they rode under 'her' bridge and out of sight. Further down the towpath, a woman in a mobility buggy had paused to chat to a fisherman and, as she did so, a dragonfly alighted for a moment on her shoulder.

But it was the canal itself that really caught Anna's attention. The clear water sparkled in the sunshine between brightly coloured boats of all shapes and sizes. Two girls whizzed by paddling bright orange canoes and, in the other direction, a canal boat chugged past, with a solar panel on its roof, a little windmill on top turning in the breeze and a young boy standing in the bow, rope in hand, waiting to moor up outside the lock. While his mother at the tiller steered past the canoeists, she shouted a joke to his father who was jogging along the towpath while their dog bounded beside him barking excitedly. Beyond 'her' bridge, where a young woman was repairing the brickwork, Anna could see a little shop with a garden leading down to the canal and around the gate into the garden grew wild roses. People were sitting in the garden drinking tea and eating ice creams.

'This looks great,' said Anna, 'so many people enjoying the canal. When is this?'

'Well,' said the water woman, 'we are looking into the future now, to 2030. A large part of the canal restoration is complete and Stroud is once more an important canal town, although now people travel the canals for pleasure and to relax rather than for work and trade.'

'Wow,' said Anna, 'I'll be 26 in 2030. I wonder what I'll be doing then.' And for a moment she was sad thinking of her father shouting at her that she would never make anything of her life. But then she looked up at the water woman who was smiling and stopped worrying.

Once more the horse turned and they trotted back – back to the hill, back down the half-familiar paths until they reached the Stroud Subscription Rooms. It was still misty.

'This is where I must leave you Anna,' said the water woman. 'You don't need to worry, your life will go well and you will play a part in the canal's future.'

And with that, she and the fine black horse simply disappeared. The mist cleared and Anna was once more sitting surrounded by shops and traffic waiting for her friends.

Well, after that, life for Anna was never quite the same. She didn't know exactly what she wanted to do but she did know it would involve the canal and, when she left school, she trained as a bricklayer.

When Anna was 26 years old, in 2030, she got her perfect job – restoring old bridges and other brickwork on the canals. One afternoon she glanced up from her work and thought she caught a glimpse of a black horse with two riders – a white-haired woman and a young girl – emerge from between the trees onto the towpath. She blinked and they were gone. Anna shook her head and smiled.

NOTES

Anna's favourite bridge is one near Stroud on the Thames and Severn canal. When Anna chooses the 'distant past' path she is taken back to the canal in 1835, almost fifty years after it opened, when it was in its heyday.

The 'recent past' path leads Anna to the canal in 1972, forty years after it was officially abandoned and just before the restoration programme – which has made such great strides forward in recent years – began. At that time the canal was a forgotten and dismal place.

The 'future path' guides Anna to the Thames and Severn in 2030, when the second phase of the restoration programme has been completed and its goal of 'inclusive community engagement' has been realised.

Bibliography

Burton, M., *Life on the Canal* (Pitkin Publishing: Stroud, 2013).

Carter, B., *Gunpowder Tunnel* (Hamish Hamilton: London, 1958).

Cotswold Canals Trust, *Life around and about Saul Junction: Gateway to the World* (CCT: Stroud, 2011).

Cotswold Canals Trust, *The Story of Brimscombe Port: where Thames and Severn met* (CCT: Stroud, 2010).

Cotswold Canals Trust, *An Introduction to the Cotswold Canals: Stroudwater Navigation and Thames & Severn Canal* (CCT: Stroud, 2009).

Eglinton, E., *The last of the Sailing Coasters: Reminiscences and Observations of the Days in the Severn Trows, Coasting Ketches and Schooners* (HMSO: 1982).

Green, C., *Severn Traders: The West Country Trows and Trowmen* (Black Dwarf Publications: Lydney, 1999).

Greenhill, B., 'Severn Trows: A Vanished Craft', *Gloucestershire Countryside,* April 1939 (Gloucestershire Archives).

Handford, M., *The Stroudwater Canal: A History* (Amberley Publishing: Stroud, 2013).

Handford, M., *The Stroudwater Canal* (Alan Sutton: Gloucester, 1979).

Household, H., *The Thames & Severn Canal* (David & Charles: Newton Abbot, 1969).

Kempley, J., *In the Wake of the Flower of Gloster* (Ronald Crowhurst, 2004).

Morton Nance, R., 'Trows Past and Present', *The Mariner's Mirror,* July 1912 (Gloucestershire Archives).

Poole, J., *Saul Adam* (Thornhill Press: Gloucester, 1973).

Roberts, T., *A Canal Walk through Stroud* (Stroudwater, Thames & Severn Canal Trust Ltd: Stroud, 1982).

Rolt, L.T.C., *Narrow Boat* (The History Press: Stroud, 2014).

Temple Thurston, E., *The Flower of Gloster* (David & Charles: Newton Abbot, 1968).

Tucker, J., *The Stroudwater Navigation: A Social History* (Tempus: Stroud, 2003).

INDEX

Society *for* Storytelling

Since 1993, The Society for Storytelling has championed the ancient art of oral storytelling and its long and honourable history – not just as entertainment, but also in education, health, and inspiring and changing lives. Storytellers, enthusiasts and academics support and are supported by this registered charity to ensure the art is nurtured and developed throughout the UK.

Many activities of the Society are available to all, such as locating storytellers on the Society website, taking part in our annual National Storytelling Week at the start of every February, purchasing our quarterly magazine Storylines, or attending our Annual Gathering – a chance to revel in engaging performances, inspiring workshops, and the company of like-minded people.

You can also become a member of the Society to support the work we do. In return, you receive free access to Storylines, discounted tickets to the Annual Gathering and other storytelling events, the opportunity to join our mentorship scheme for new storytellers, and more. Among our great deals for members is a 30% discount off titles from The History Press.

For more information, including how to join, please visit

www.sfs.org.uk